Date Due

PEACE *without* HATE

GEORGE W. NORRIS

PEACE *without* HATE

A LECTURE DELIVERED AT THE UNIVERSITY OF NEBRASKA

UNIVERSITY OF NEBRASKA PRESS
LINCOLN: 1943

 PRINTED IN THE UNITED STATES OF AMERICA AT THE PRINTING DIVISION, UNIVERSITY OF NEBRASKA.

FIRST EDITION

INTRODUCTION

AT THE REQUEST of the faculty of the University of Nebraska Senator George W. Norris delivered a lecture under the auspices of the institution at a public gathering.

The distinguished Nebraskan presented in his lecture a broad outline of the underlying principles which, in his judgment, should determine the peace to be drawn at the close of the present conflict.

Senator Norris wisely made no effort to discuss the individual complicated problems of territorial determination, national boundaries to be established, precise formulas for the punishment of those against whom war guilt may be established, or the precise steps to be undertaken in the rehabilitation of governments and peoples within long occupied countries. The wisdom of such a course was established in the closing days of April, 1943, when the first evidence of disunity between the peoples of the United Nations made its appearance.

THE EDITOR

THE WHOLE CIVILIZED world now is interested, tremendously interested, in the peace that shall follow the war in which we are engaged.

Any peace to be fashioned by the governments and the peoples of the United Nations, of course, presupposes a victory by the United Nations. Naturally the completeness of victory will have some influence over the peace that follows—but the peace that everybody is thinking about, the peace everybody is hoping for and praying for, is a peace that shall be lasting and perpetual. It is a peace that will enable all peoples of the world to bind up their wounds and proceed upon their orderly ways of living.

The peace which came from out of the First World War is of little or no importance because it did not last. It was and is of little importance because everybody now knows that such a peace could only be the spawning ground for another world war. This impoverished, battered world of ours cannot afford the luxury and the crime of a third world war.

We should be preparing our minds now. It seems to me perfectly apparent that in reaching a peace, which shall be permanent, the American people and their allies are going to be called upon to make sacrifices as great, possibly, as any they were asked to shoulder during the war itself. They are going to be compelled to make compromises — compromises which come hard to a people of strong beliefs and convictions with definite fixed ideas of their own place in this world and the place of other nations. They are going to be called upon to remember that associated with them in this struggle are Russia, China, the British Empire and all of its dominions, those governments ruthlessly driven from their own soil, now in exile, and the peoples of the conquered nations. It will be necessary to consult them in determining permanent peace.

We must try to agree among ourselves what principles are essential to peace—what material facts are the foundation for it—and what instrumentalities must be created in order to give it permanence. That peace may not be just what we of the United States want. We may be compelled to sacrifice some of our ideas in order to bring about agreement.

As a condition to peace, it seems plain to me, the war must end, and only can end, in the unconditional surrender of the enemy. There must be no repetition of the earlier mistake of twenty-five years ago. There must be no appeasement.

There can be no negotiated peace in a war which has been accepted as a war of extermination. If we lose this struggle we recognize the inevitability of the loss of human liberties—of the imposition of human slavery—and of death to that which a free man holds dear.

THOSE TO BE CONSIDERED

So frequently it has been incomprehensible to the human mind that any human being could be so cruel as to do those things that have been done and now are being done openly and defiantly by the enemy. Those countries that have stood up longest in successful resistance—the Chinese, the Russians, and the people of the British Empire—naturally are the peoples who have suffered in war the greatest and because of their successful resistance will have the greatest voice in the drafting of the peace. Those peoples, and the American people, because their governments have spent the money and because their men have sacrificed their lives, must assuredly assume the great responsibility of leadership in the formulation of the peace.

We are not unmindful that there are many other governments and many other peoples—peoples of peaceful inclination, peoples who have made great contributions to the world, peoples who have enriched its literature, its arts, and its culture—who have been ground beneath the tyrannical heel, who have been robbed, and who are continuing to suffer greatly. Those peoples necessarily, wherever there is human compassion, and respect and admiration for the eternal virtues of life, will greatly occupy our thoughts.

Yet, through no fault of their own, through no fault of the heart but only through the failure of the flesh, they have not done what this union of nations, still resisting valiantly, has done. In the struggle that has continued since Hitler rolled through and over their lands they have not furnished the men and money to make possible the final complete defeat of Hitlerism in the world—and I speak of Hitler principally because he seems to incarnate the spirit of conquest and aggression which dominates our enemies and which symbolizes the force in this world that must be crushed and defeated.

After the enemy has surrendered unconditionally —after we have taken possession of the weapons with which he has been waging war—of the factories which have been supplying his armies—and of the materials upon which he has drawn to wage war— we shall be ready for the peace. It will not be necessary and we should not consult those who brought about this war. It will be necessary for those who brought about the end of war through complete triumph to reach agreement among themselves, and that will entail struggle.

We start at the beginning by the admission that America is only one of the contending peoples determined to defeat Hitlerism no matter how long it takes. *But unless the war continues for several years more we should be fair enough, candid enough, and honest enough to recognize that we have not suffered in the loss of young manhood to a degree comparable to some of these nations that fight by our side.*

As a prelude to peace, what is it that we fight, and why do we fight? We fight a defensive war against conceptions of racial supremacy; we fight a defensive war against lust and greed for territorial riches; we fight a defensive war because of the avowed intention of a government and a nation that looks upon itself and themselves as a superior people destined to rule.

A WAR AGAINST A PHILOSOPHY

Hitler, and other German leaders before him, taught the German people, taught the German people unfortunately, that they were the superior race; that they were entitled to rule the world and that in a plan of domination all other nations must be subservient to their purpose and to their will. To establish their superiority it remained only for Hitler to take that step that sanctioned deception in the written and spoken word—in the treaty and the covenant—and the tactics of murder, robbery, and rape in the strategy of the battlefield.

Now the question may arise: How about Germany's allies?

Japan has been a modern nation for a period of little more than seventy-five years. Its ancient, primitive, barbaric, militaristic philosophy survives and dominates its thought. For generations the Japanese have been taught the glory of battle; in it was the satisfaction of earthly existence, and the fulfillment of spiritual aspirations.

The Italian people under the rule of Mussolini have been taught that war is good, that war is the heritage of a strong people seeking to establish a place for itself. Under Mussolini the Italian people were dazzled with the vision of the restoration of a great empire and with a renaissance of the glory and greatness of ancient Rome.

SPIRIT OF REVENGE

I know that it is human, and I know that there arises in every human breast a feeling of revenge and hatred against any enemy that has cast aside any pretense to honor, and that has eliminated from daily life the instincts of justice which civilization has developed. Their justice is the rule of the sword; not the rule of reason or of the mind. I know it is most human that in all this suffering and misery the cry should go up that many of the leaders of these aggressor nations should be confined to prison for the remainder of their lives and that some of these leaders should pay with their lives. It is so natural for violence to beget violence; for hate to breed hate; and for murder to produce murder.

While this is natural, *restraint of the passions so justly aroused by what has happened, restraint of the hate so naturally engendered by what has taken place, restraint of the determination for revenge so common to human flesh is one of the sacrifices we must impose upon ourselves.* We must remember that if we are to have a perpetual peace we must not establish, under any circumstances, a rule of government that practices precisely the same things and is guilty of exactly the same wrongs that we charge against our enemies. A permanent peace will not come out of any peace that is framed in hate and dedicated to posterity with the spirit of vengeance.

What is necessary in order to achieve a perpetual peace? It is not difficult, it seems to me, with all the experience that is back of us to tell us what that is.

TAKING AWAY WEAPONS

As a first step we must require our enemies to disarm. To my mind, it is absolutely essential that the weapons which enable Hitler, and the German people under him, Mussolini and the Italian people under him, the Japanese emperor and the Japanese people under him to wage war, must be taken from them and they must be prevented from fashioning them again. We must not only require the enemy to disarm but we must provide in the treaty of peace a method of making that disarmament which comes at the time of unconditional surrender a permanent disarmament in these countries that have been so hungry for war.

I may have an exaggerated idea of the importance

of disarmament. But an unarmed man never rushes into trouble or seeks trouble. An unarmed government, and an unarmed people, never strut around with a chip upon their shoulders picking a fight. It seems to me that the predominating and the great preliminary step in the attainment of a perpetual peace is the outlawing of those weapons that make war possible.

Every armed ship which flies the flag of these aggressor nations must be destroyed. Every submarine must be sunk and sent to the bottom of the sea. Every gun that spits fire and steel must be made worthless. Every factory within these nations that dream and plan of war, every factory that produces the ammunition and explosives and weapons for their armies, must be demolished completely. If it is the desire of the world that this peace shall be perpetual there can be no half-way measures in disarmament. All of the heartache, the misery, the destruction of property, the sacrifice of manhood, and the mountainous debts of nations can be and must be charged to the half-hearted steps taken to disarm those nations that caused war.

Memory is short. A generation comes into being quickly. The babies, who in their innocence know nothing of the causes of war or the physical symbols of war, are the men and women of tomorrow who realize little of the inevitable evil of the weapons that were a part of the years of their babyhood. This generation under Hitler that has borne the burden of his war either was born during the last war largely or after the last war. It had no incentive for disarming. No perpetual peace will be possible with these surviving generations of Germans, Italians, and Japanese without the condition of disarmament.

It will not be difficult to seize the ships that are armed, the submarines, the tanks, and the airplanes. It will not be difficult to compel the surrender of the guns. It will not be difficult to demolish the munitions plants. But that is only a part of it, although what remains is not so difficult of itself.

It will not require a very large standing army to enforce disarmament in these aggressor countries. In my judgment after the lapse of a few years the burden of policing these countries will disappear. A people once disarmed, completely disarmed, without the vestige of weapons with which to fight, are subject absolutely to the police power over them—police power that is armed—although numerically much less than the power that is disarmed. And I believe that once the people of Germany, and that once the people of Italy, once the people of Japan are relieved of the burden of armaments which their governments have imposed upon them they themselves will accept disarmament as a blessing.

THOSE YET TO BE BORN

In thinking of this peace, in all of our thought and deliberations upon it, we must think not only of the world as it is today but of the world that will be—the world in which people not yet born will live. All of us here now will pass beyond. We will be gone and the men and women who then will be on earth, the men and women who will take charge of its affairs will be the men and women who are slumbering today in the womb of time. I like to think of this peace as a peace not only for us, old and young, but as a peace for the unborn generations numbering hundreds of millions, innocent as they are of any part in this crime of today.

Only by contemplation of the future—only by thinking in terms of endless time—will we find the strength, the inspiration, and the vision to restrain the natural impulses of our nature and to give us strength to forego revenge upon enemies who do not deserve mercy. They do not deserve mercy or compassion, but this peace is not to strike a balance between the evil men who precipitated this war and those immediate sufferers from it, but it is a peace which must reckon with the needs of endless time.

We may find in Japan a special problem. Japan is of the East; we are of the West. Back of Japan is an unbroken record of thirty years of conquest on the Asiatic mainland and the islands of the Pacific. Back of Japan is a tradition of self-denial of the ordinary necessities of life in the development of a military machine to establish Japanese supremacy in the Pacific; but once beaten, beaten thoroughly, a small army in Japan can disarm the Japanese completely and thoroughly. Once stripped of guns, cartridges, ships, and bombs, Japan can be kept disarmed. We like to think that in every one of these countries there are people, possibly millions of people, who do not share their government's attitude in this war and who do not sympathize with their government's purposes but who remain as speechless as the dead because to speak out freely the sentiment that is in their heart would mean certain death.

I know that it will be suggested early in all discussions of peace by many good people here in the United States and elsewhere: "If you are going to disarm the enemy, why not disarm ourselves?"

We should be practical. The ideal condition of this world will be reached when every nation has disarmed. But in any practical thinking we cannot reach that ideal condition now; it is impossible.

I am persuaded disarmament ultimately will take care of itself. In my humble opinion, gradually as the need for arms grows less, as the peaceful inclinations grow stronger, the spirit of armament will wear itself out and fade away. Under a new government in Japan I think that with sufficient passage of time her own people, allowed to speak, gladly would subscribe to disarmament. It means more comforts for them. It means less poverty for them. It means more hope for the mothers of sons.

THE HIGHEST DUTY

Weapons are meant for war. Those who live and through their lives become imbued with the idea that war is the fulfillment of their destiny, the destiny of a superior people, in the attainment of which nothing must be permitted to stand, not even murder, are those who furnish the world with a spirit of aggression and force. A rising generation properly taught would not be taught that the highest duty of a man is to serve a military machine in order that the government under which he lives may dominate and enslave people.

If Germany, Japan, and Italy were to be disarmed completely in this fashion, then the only dominating nations of the world that would be armed are Russia, China, Great Britain, and ourselves. We know little of Russia. We recognize in Russia a great gallantry in the defense of her soil and of her institutions. We recognize in China the elements of true greatness. We recognize in ourselves the absence of any desire to exploit the peoples or territories of other nations of the world. We know that in the case of Russia, when Japan moved into Manchuria, it was the Russian government that joined the American government in protest against that act of aggression. We know the long tradition of the Chinese people for peace.

We must have something of faith in ourselves and in those that fight by our side if we are to achieve a perpetual peace. And we have material foundation for that faith. We have either the largest or one of the largest armies in the world. We have the greatest productive capacity at this time of any nation engaged in war. There is no other nation in the world outside of ourselves and those who are our enemies that today presents to the world any danger whatever of military supremacy. I advocate this not only because I believe it is the highest way in which to bring about this peace but I believe it is the only practical way through which we may reach permanent, perpetual peace.

NO HUGE INDEMNITIES

We must not as a second condition demand of the defeated aggressor nations the payment of the enormous debts which have been saddled upon the world by this war. That debt is so great—so stupendous—that it will require the combined labors of all the peoples in the world to discharge it.

Only as a matter of common sense we should recognize that no nation or no three nations have the productive capacities or the resources to discharge it. We should require of the defeated aggressor nations the reasonable payment of anything that they can pay. We should not place ourselves in a position of demanding the impossible. When we do, then we ourselves write a peace that cannot be fulfilled in human expectations.

When this war is over Japan, Italy, and Germany will be prostrate. Their farms will be devastated, their cities in ruins or in partial ruins, and their millions of people either dead or so physically exhausted they no longer can struggle on. They will not at the time of their exhaustion be able to make any great payment. We must not at the time of our victory expect the defeated enemies to pay us immediately a part of the debt which they owe us, or any part of that debt at an early date, because we know in our hearts that again would represent an impossibility.

They must be given time to recover. They must be given an opportunity to recuperate in the individual sense; they must have a chance to rehabilitate their industries, to restore their homes, and to take up again the occupations that furnish them a livelihood.

REPUDIATE THEIR DEBTS

It does seem to me that we should require of these defeated aggressor nations that their governments repudiate all of the debts incurred in this war which they initiated. There are two good reasons for this. First, it would have a tendency to cause the financier, who furnishes the money for war and profits by war, to hesitate before he loans money to any nation that sets out upon conquering the world. Second, it would enable these aggressor nations to pay a larger sum into the indemnity chest, if it is to be called that, reimbursing the allied nations for the losses which they have sustained.

There are many other things which might be desirable in a treaty of peace. They may be difficult of attainment or impossible of achievement. We read so often of the desirability of re-establishing the trade opportunities in the world. We are told so frequently that it is the tariff barriers erected by governments that stifle and strangle the people and contribute to war. Do you know where you would find opposition to an alteration of the tariff barrier? It would be right here at home. When you say "tariff" to Congress, suggesting its elimination or modification downward, you have a fight on your hands right off. Right or wrong, desirable or undesirable, it is one of those impossibilities. I think that we should concede that so far as possible the basis of permanent and perpetual peace is to enable every government to take care of its own internal affairs.

So many of those obstacles of immense stature today will disappear the nearer the approach to peace comes. Its practical problems are wide and diversified and complicated; its principles simple and few.

Again I emphasize that we must remove all thoughts of revenge from our hearts. We must be the Good Samaritan. We must feed the starving and clothe the naked. We will be called upon to do that, as we now know, because when this war is over, devastation and ruin will cover much of the occupied countries and virtually all of the enemy territory—much of three continents.

Those nations at war or in slavery as a result of war, with the exception of the United States, will emerge on the verge of starvation. In furnishing them food we are not doing it in the spirit of goodness but in the hope of restoring a tortured world. We are doing it in the belief it is the road to permanent peace. We want these nations as friends. We want the conquered nations to be friends of our government because through such friendship for the American government, and for the allied governments, the only path to a leadership for peace is prepared.

We have practical examples of what hatred does. We have indisputable proof that nursed, it sows the seeds of another war. We have before our own eyes the evidence that hatred planted in the minds of little children will survive there as long as they live to constitute a potential cause of war. There is the case of two neighbors—France and Germany—with a searing hatred of seventy years between them, a hatred handed down from father to son. It began in war; it evaded any attempts in the formulation of the peace that followed that war; it gave birth to still another war.

So those who say that we are going to get even with our enemies, honest in the expression of that sentiment and patriotic as may be the prompting for it, are nevertheless wrong, and eternally wrong. *The burden of the peace we want is the burden of helping our enemy to his feet.*

Can we do this? Can we succeed in driving from our hearts all ideas of hate and revenge, or are we going to say, as one of foreign blood who completed his naturalization steps in this country some time ago said to me in a letter: "When we get this victory, I believe in taking an eye for an eye and a tooth for a tooth."

AGE-OLD LESSONS

A thousand years of war has said that same thing. It rings from the battlefields of all the continents where men met in armed conflict and died.

If we are thinking of a perpetual peace, perhaps there is no better commandment than the one which says: "It is more blessed to give than to receive."

There is no more beautiful, no sweeter story than that of the Good Samaritan. That joy that came to the man injured and crippled was not as great as the joy that came to the heart of the Samaritan who helped and who came to help at a time when help was needed. I cannot other than feel that the heart of the human race will be chastened and softened by the fire and hell through which it must pass in this ordeal of war.

A millionaire of Great Britain who had been driven into a shelter with his child met there beneath the surface of the earth a beggar with his child and a laboring man with his family. In their minds they had been enemies. Today they have seen each other's struggles. The laboring man gets the viewpoint of the millionaire; the beggar comes to his relief. The millionaire goes to the relief of the poor man. They become in all of this torture the brothers God intended them to be. The millionaire sees and recognizes that all of his wealth only puts him on an equality with the lowest human being in his country. The brotherly spirit springs up.

The Russian people, it is estimated, have lost ten million people in men, women, and children. Some have died on the battlefield; many others of starvation. Out of all of Russia's suffering has come a spirit of unity and common purpose greater than that implanted by governmental design.

China, innocent of any wrong against Japan, innocent of any intention to do harm to others, has lost millions of her people—some of them dead by crimes that are unspeakable—and yet in this torture the Chinese people have been brought closer together.

I believe that nations like China and Great Britain and Russia, having gone through this ordeal of fire, having been purified on the altar of self-sacrifice, are going to be a little more humane when this war is over. They are going to be a little more anxious to extend a hand of fellowship.

We in America have not experienced that yet. Here on our own soil we have not gone through all the agony that war brings when war advances directly to the fireside. But we also have changed in our hearts and in our souls. We feel different here at home than we once did. There is not one pattern existing today that was in existence twenty years ago. We are less divided into classes, less conscious of those barriers that formerly existed between groups here in the United States. If we are to follow our own pretensions to any degree, proclaim the standards that we ourselves have heralded to the world, we will reach the conclusion at the peace table that we will not enslave our enemies but help them to their feet.

NOT THE SAME ALLIES

It has been said that in this treaty of peace we should provide for something like the League of Nations to keep the peace of the world. It is then assumed, of course, that all of these nations of Europe will become a part of and participate in the development and the establishment of such a tribunal. While I would like to see a family of nations when the war is over, and I hope that it will come about, in a practical sense I fear that it will not be realized. It is not to be expected that the nations who fight Japan for instance—Great Britain, China, Holland, and the United States—who furnish the money and the men to insure that victory—will permit the terms of peace to be made by nations that had no part in it.

There will probably be, it seems to me, two treaties of peace. One will deal with Germany and Italy and their satellite nations in Europe. The other will deal with Japan and will be drawn by the nations engaged in war against Japan.

We ought not to try to put into a peace treaty thousands of things that will not be a part of international relations in the event of disarmament. We should endeavor to restrict all efforts to the simple fundamentals; we should attempt to stick to the main principles, those principles that promise most to end war.

It will take years before the nations of the world again are free and the actual building of a new world will have begun. I would like to see this good old world start out on the theory that war is going to end. In my judgment disarmament will end it. In my judgment the peace of the world is going to depend upon us and our allies when we have attained victory over our enemies. When that victory has been obtained, then the only vestige of dispute existing in the world will have disappeared and surrendered, and the opportunity then is present to build a new world with a heritage of a perpetuity of peace. That which we are fighting, that which always leads to war is the rule of force.

We shall be true to the faith, we pledge that faith, we give voice to the faith that we are fighting for human freedom, that we are fighting to relieve the world of military tyrants. If that is true, out of the intelligence and heart of men we shall carve a peace in the image of eternity.

This book is printed from

Linotype Granjon

and

hand-set Kenntonian type

on

antique laid paper

The frontispiece is an original portrait

by

ENIT KAUFMAN

UNIVERSITY OF NEBRASKA PRESS

LINCOLN